Leo's Sleepover
A Diabetic Story

March

WRITTEN BY
Dave Colquhoun

ILLUSTRATED BY
Stacey Kissock

ISBN-13: 978-1-0695468-0-7

      Also available as an e-book!

Published by Haystack Publishing

British Columbia

Cover design by Chelsea Jackson and Stacey Kissock

Typeset by Chelsea Jackson

Edited by Jackson Writing and Editing, LLC

Dedicated to my two kids,
Chris and Kaylee.

To Devin and Taylor.

Leo burst into the house. "Dad! Can I have a sleepover at Finn's tonight?"

Leo's dad frowned. "I'm afraid not, Leo. You don't know how to take care of your diabetes yourself yet."

Leo threw his backpack at the empty couch and stomped out of the room.

Leo's dad poked his head into Leo's room. "Finn is more than welcome to sleep here tonight."

"Will I ever be able to have a sleepover at his house?" Leo asked.

"Let's help you take more responsibility for your diabetes first, then we can talk about it."

The front door flew open.
Finn rushed in
with his sleeping
bag flowing
behind him
like a

superhero cape.

"Let's make a
blanket fort!"
Leo said.

They crawled into their finished fort and gazed up at the twinkling lights.

"When can you have a sleepover at my house?" Finn asked.

Leo sighed. "I need to learn how to take care of my diabetes myself first. Someone still has to remind me to check my blood sugar."

"Why do you need to check your blood sugar?"

"If I have too much insulin in my body, my blood sugar might be low, which is dangerous. I'll need sugar right away, like juice or candy."

"What is diabetes anyway?" Finn asked.

"My body doesn't produce insulin like yours."

Insulin moves sugar into the cells to help give the body fuel. People inject insulin into their bodies using a needle to help their bodies get the energy they need to function.

Leo sat in the school cafeteria and checked his blood sugar.

Finn slid into the seat next to him. "What are you doing?"

"I'm checking my blood sugar. I do it before every meal, so I know how much insulin I need to give myself."

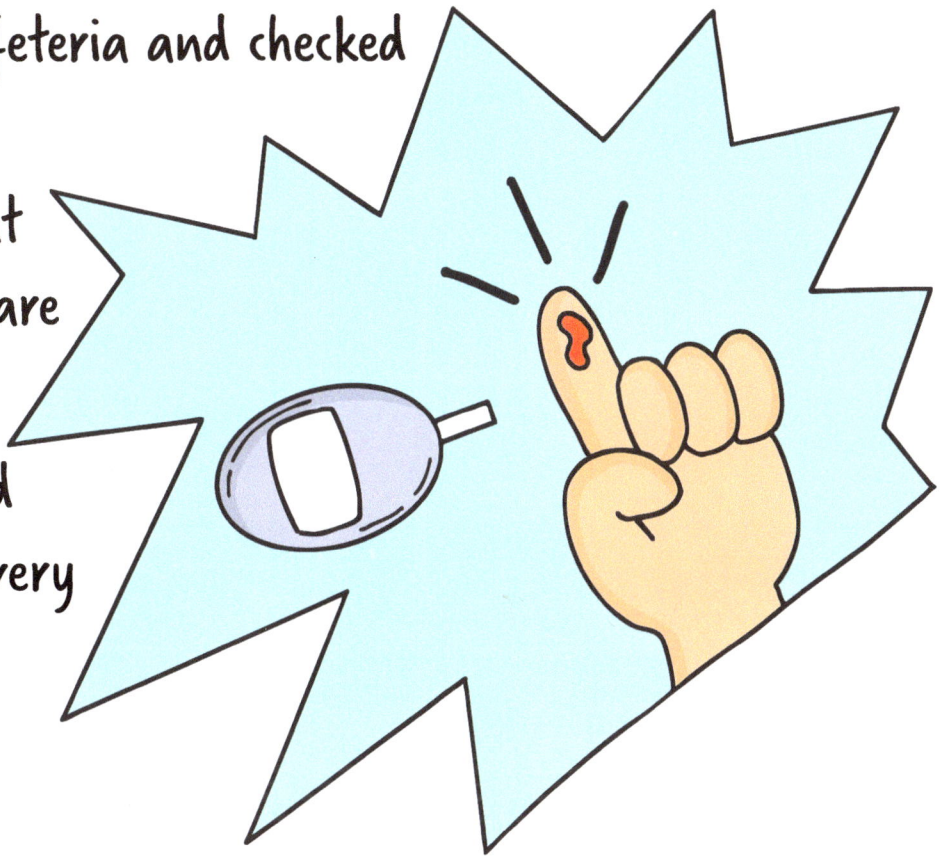

Diabetics check their blood sugar by poking a finger to get a tiny drop of blood. They put the blood on a strip and use a small meter to see how much sugar is in it.

"What happens if your blood sugar is too low or too high?"
Finn asked with a mouthful of stuffed-crust pizza.

"I feel tired or sometimes angry and confused," Leo explained as he put his supplies back in his backpack.

Like a car, bodies need fuel to move. When people have low blood sugar, it's like their car runs out of gas. They might feel shaky, sweaty, or dizzy.

"What else do you have in that bag?" Finn asked.

"My emergency supplies like insulin, a juice box, and candy. I take it everywhere."

"And what's that thing on your belt?"

Leo looked down at his constant companion.

"Oh, that's my insulin pump. It sends insulin through a tube into my body."

The insulin pump site has a small needle. The site and insulin are changed to a new location on the stomach every three to four days.

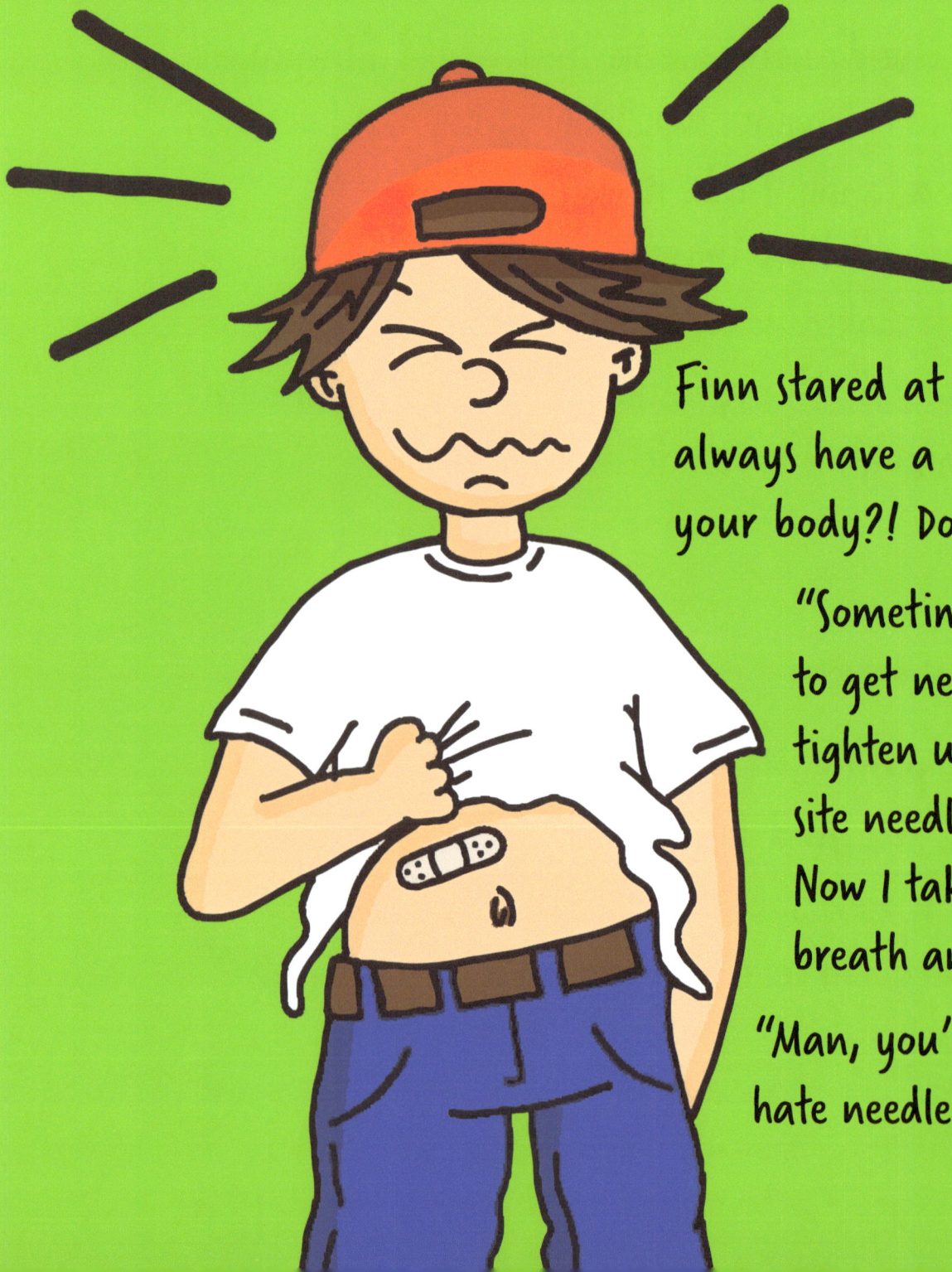

Finn stared at Leo. "You always have a needle in your body?! Does it hurt?"

"Sometimes. I used to get nervous and tighten up before my site needle changed. Now I take a deep breath and relax."

"Man, you're brave. I hate needles!"

Finn and Leo dumped their trash in the garbage.

"Will your diabetes go away?" Finn asked.

"Not unless scientists find a cure. I hope they do soon. I don't want other kids to go through what I've gone through."

TRAS

"It's a big job to take care of my diabetes. Our teacher, education assistants, and my parents help me control my diabetes. I'm learning to do more and more by myself. If I get good, my parents might let me have a sleepover at your house!"

That afternoon, Finn pulled out an invitation to his birthday party.

BIRTHDAY PARTY

FOR __LEO__

DATE __MARCH 15TH__

PLACE __FINN'S HOUSE__

__IT'S A SLEEPOVER!__

"I'd love to come, Finn! Let me talk to my parents," Leo said. He high-fived Finn. He had two weeks to show his parents he could be responsible with his diabetes.

At dinner, Leo said, "Dad, I really want to go to Finn's birthday sleepover."

Dad spooned spaghetti onto his plate. "Then you need to check your blood sugar without being reminded. And know what to do if it's too high or too low," Dad added.

As the sleepover day approached, Leo's excitement grew. He worked hard to consistently care for his diabetes and received permission from his dad to attend the sleepover party at Finn's.

March

						1	2
3	4	5	6	7	8	9	
10	11	12	13	14	15 FINN'S PARTY!	16	
17	18	19	20	21	22	23	
24 31	25	26	27	28	29	30	

Finally, Friday arrived, and Leo packed his insulin, juice box, trusty backpack, and sleepover things.

When Finn answered the door, he held two of their favorite superhero figures.

"Let's save the planet!" Finn said.

"Right after I check my blood sugar," Leo said.

Author

Dave Colquhoun

Dave Colquhoun has been a teacher in Trail, British Columbia, for many years and a dad for even longer! He loves helping kids learn and wanted to write a book that makes type 1 diabetes easier to understand. Dave has two children, Christopher and Kaylee. When he's not teaching or coaching, you might find him walking his border collie, Lola, or hitting the golf course.

Illustrator

Stacey Kissock

Stacey Kissock has always loved to draw and enjoys using art to relax and be creative. She's been married to her husband, Darrin, for seventeen years and is a proud mom to two great kids, Devin and Taylor. Stacey loves camping, watching her kids play ball, and spending time with her family and their dog, Rocky.

This book is a special way for her to share her love of drawing with others.

Enjoy the book?
Please leave a
review on Amazon
or Goodreads and
share it with your
friends!

www.ingramcontent.com/pod-product-compliance
Lightning Source LLC
LaVergne TN
LVHW072115070426
835510LV00002B/62